FRAGMENTS OF LIFE

- The inner beauty

FRAGMENTS OF LIFE
- The inner beauty

Poems & layout by Ulla Conrad, www.ullaconrad.com
Photos by Semko Balcerski, www.semko.dk

1. udgave, 1. oplag

ISBN: 978-87-4300-400-4
Forlag: BoD – Books on Demand, Hellerup, Danmark
Tryk: BoD – Books on Demand, Norderstedt, Tyskland, 2023,
www.bod.dk

Ulla Conrad

FRAGMENTS OF LIFE
- The inner beauty

81 poems

Previous releases by the same author:

"Vertraue der Nacht Geheimnisse an. Gedichte",
Digte, Frieling Verlag, Berlin, 1999

"De Grønne Skyggers Land. Skitser, digte, haiku fra Japan",
Digte, Forlaget Ravnerock, 2012

„Bladværk - haiku-inspirerede årstidsord",
Haiku digte, Forlaget Ravnerock, 2019

„Jorden ånder - livscyklusdigte",
Digte, Forlaget Ravnerock, 2019

"Gendarmstien - 84 km vandring langs den dansk-tyske grænse",
Vandrebog, Forlaget Hovedland, 2020

"Puder af mos - japanske meditationer gennem det danske år",
Essays og digte, Forlaget Ravnerock, 2020

"Marskstien med mere. Vandringer ved Vadehavet",
Vandrebog, Forlaget Hovedland, 2021

„Nordkyststien. Den Danske Riviera mellem Helsingør og Hundested",
Vandrebog, Forlaget Hovedland, 2022

Contents

I

"The Fragments of Life"
- the inner beauty
(Exhibition)
2003

1.

Arriving at the edge of the world
who would have expected
glimpses of beauty
glimpses of wonder
questioning existence
as it is

every blink of my eye
changes a view
changes pattern in colour
behaviour and minds
in all of us

in me -

2.

Senses invaded
not knowing where to look first
pleasure in all places
all in all illusory
misleading

you think you know
what you know and still
so much - there is so much
you don't know that
you don't know

wonder
what that is -

3.

If impermanence is
permanent
everything changes
and comes back as itself
or something else

Déjà-vu's are not as
strange anymore and not
without meaning

listening
a world opens and takes you
away without a chance
of resisting -

4.

Recognising in glimpses
happiness unhappiness
heaven and hell
yin and yang
accepting living IT
having faith

years have passed
and you might find yourself
as a part of a world
of mediterranean forest pine trees
smelling rotten leaves
feeling soft ground
under your feet
not knowing what time of year
what time at all
because time
is not -

5.

Endless wondering about

why I
smell the scent of white flowers
in the ground which no one can see

why I
feel the nutty taste of beechnuts
between my teeth
crumbling dry and warm
like the autumn around me
meant for squirrels but not me

why I
sense the suns last beams
still warming the skin
though millions of miles away
being me
being a part of all this

only a part -

6.

From far away sounds screaming
and apart from music
I see the face of new life emerging
from the dark
drifting to the surface
becoming part of the world

now there are two, then
there are hundreds
there are millions of things
which are love
which are life
which are everything

and more -

7.

Fragments of life
small bits and parts of a lifetime
flickering around
in the void of the mind
remembering turning them around
to see from all sides
reflecting from inside to outside
and back -

8.

A labyrinth of mirrors
is what I walk into
an illusive mirage
a fantasy, an aberration
making delusions arise
mental deceptions
false impressions

what is real
what is left

I don't know
anymore -

9.

What I have been looking for
in the beginning
is a memory just
lost

much better though
this
supreme greatness
and for the eye
optical wonders

me
caught by surprise

left
with astonishment
and admiration

breathless -

10.

Majestic beauty emerges
in details of nature

covers the face of my mind
decorates the surface
may hide something lying beneath

forming a pattern
composed by a number of elements

created repeated
symmetric

still in control -

11.

Days and months
and years go by
forming the rhythm
of life

moving changing
appearing in patterns
as a beat

a never-ending
pulse -

12.

Close your eyes
and take a look
at the unseen
listen
to the unspoken

behind shadows
there may be dreams
there may be glimmering lights
in vicious circles, captured
wandering around in the future
and searching for the past

behind silence
there may be voices constantly talking
to themselves
and you
merely a stage
for their show -

II

New poems for
"The Fragments of Life"
2003-2007

13.

There is no reason for
why you should
hide from yourself
run from yourself
or have wicked ideas about
who you should be

stay and
face the fear

then you will find
green fields of barley
wind in the grass
and a fox playing

then you will find IT
the secret
the sacred
in it all -

14.

The night has just gone

and a blackbird has started
the morning with song

a fox is playing in the dim light
searching for mice

your mind can enjoy
falling and rising
wondering again
about life
with a light mind

right now -

15.

A little silver fish
breaks through the surface
of the sea, then disappears

silence

though beautiful
this is a question of survival
without thinking
the fish does what is has to do
without questioning
it acts

a closer look
at human beings shows
we often are making cloudy decisions
and creating confusion -

but isn't all we want
to survive and
to be loved?

16.

Being born
being given a new life
in the endless
order of lives

a new chance
every time

being with IT
being a stand for love

being one with
this blue planet and
all its sentient beings

breathing
and go on breathing
beyond life and death -

17.

Just minutes ago
ocean and sky were one

clouds like blue coloured
mountain silhouettes
melted into the waves below -

but then a sudden sight
a crack has opened
and the sun shines through
a blood flooded scar
a red coloured burning ball
in the sky

an enlightened sky -

18.

"Do you see it?"
"What?"
"The moon..."

The moon

it catches me running
casting light
on the path of my mind
revealing my ego
pulling faces at me
fighting with the natural self
trying to survive

in moonlight -

19.

The former glory
of an old house
an old garden's romance
souls buried in rosebuds
and small suns dancing
against the stream
of ancient
consciousness

the taste of a raspberry
explodes in my mouth
and I am one with cosmos

for a while -

20.

Lost track in search for
a shoe a number too small

what was it
that I got up for
I ask the wren beside me
mumbling about
him being the king of birds
and that he was told
what to do
- and was happy about it
was free

burning rosemary
it lights up green
and disappears -

21.

Whatever the wren
might say about it
it is true
that rosemary is burning
the way to my heart

oleander blooms on the outside
waiting to take over
to heal the whole body
to save it

lights are going crazy
out there in the barley
taking off leaving
swirling around and throwing
themselves into life
like the call of the night owl
frozen glass in echoes
of eternity -

22.

A whole world of thoughts
taking form
complex constructed ideas
mind games questioning
if you are good enough
or constantly trying to look good
in the eyes of others
wondering how to survive
smiling

don't be too hard on yourself
remember that there is
more than this
if you connect
to cosmos
to the micro cosmos
inside yourself -

23.

Calm on the outside
functioning perfectly
living up to standards

on the inside a voice
is questioning all this

are you good enough
is there more somewhere
should you be you
are you lovable
are your dreams worth living -

and now I know
the answer is yes
and yes
and yes -

III

Poems inspired by Rumi

2008

24.

After swimming
in Rumi's words
when you feel the taste
of a universal truth

it is like the scent
of a forbidden fruit
you desperately long to
take a bite of
it is a taste
we long for
we like to experience

and then
after that
we can die -

25.

Rumi's longing
for something bigger
accepted

and then still
the constant absence of
what you really long for
being one with non-being
non-doing*

remembering
praising emptiness
to create from
in the here and now

in nothing, no thing
in everything, every thing -

** chin. wu wei = non action, a state of personal harmony*

26.

My friend
what we know is hidden
and when the sun in the morning
shines on dewdrops in the grass
we smile
illuminated
from the inside

we smile
at the feeling
of being connected
with everything
the recognition
of what IT is
the secret
the sacred
the humility we feel
when being present
in every second
every now -

27.

The sea glittering
so still without a wave
an early August morning
the light filling me up
just as I am filled up
by uplifting words
which Rumi uttered
700 years ago

a golden red tread
lighting up like hidden rubies
in the mountains
shining through everything

concentrating to
small golden pills

a chain of enlightened souls
through infinite
spiral shaped
timeless time -

28.

Jagged little pill
words popping up
in my head this morning
in the ocean of oceans
but why nobody knows

golden pill going jagged
the first title on the 1995 tape
by Alanis Morissette
a title You oughta know
a hint towards truth
in myself
Ironic another title
life's irony
the inner smile
see how small you are
still comforting
next title You learn
you learn
I will

thank you -

29.

Wondrous reality
a floating word
in a floating world

what I see is not
what you see
what about just seeing
isn't it enough
to honour and accept
what is created
so powerfully
so perfectly well?

IV

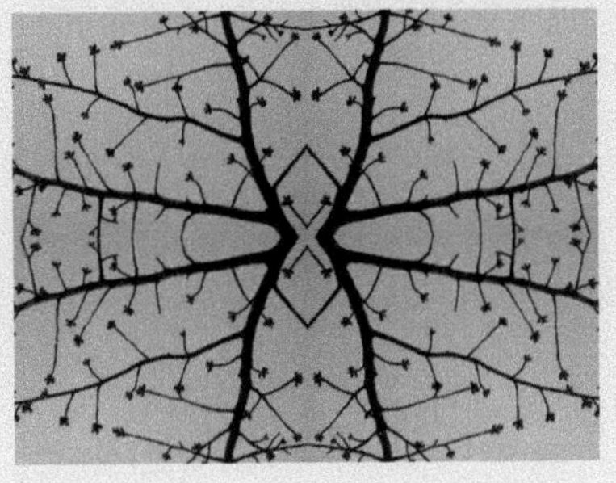

Poems inspired by
tao, zen and Eckhart Tolle
2008-2009

30.

Dancing through the cosmos
celebrating each season
and being in the beauty
of the moment
of each now

dancing through the cosmos
with one foot on a cloud each
with one finger on each flower in sight
tasting each detail with your eye
with your heart truthfully searching
inwards

look exactly at
how things are
look with honest eyes
rather twice than once

listen to the quietness
inside you
and tell me
how you are -

31.

Atom by atom
planet by planet

will you help me
counting the stars
one by one

and colouring the sky
bright again?

32.

Don't look so worried
look up in the skies

life is like a game to be played
every sign for you to be searched
maybe followed maybe not

everything is there for you to be
enjoyed and smiled at

everything is your choice to be handled
in one way or another
really - your choice

and that again you can choose

to be a burden or
a game -

33.

Breathing slowly
breathing calm
into the big void
below your navel
breathing with that
sending the inner smile
to that
and to where it can heal

breathing out
relax
the pain will melt
freeing energy
to do

what you want -

34.

Bird-flocks landing
chirping
in the hedges, filtered
in and disappearing
foraging on berries
sitting like beautiful pearls
at the bottom of the sea
like water fleas hovering in water
dancing living in the cosmos
flowing with the flow
being one

who is watching
what is this
really -

35.

The yellow aspens
the red-golden cherry leaves
burning in the valley
watched carefully from above
by the buzzard
looking for today´s dinner

only the mind can call this
beauty

for the rest of nature
things just are -

36.

This stone lying there
at the entrance of the forest
a broad and smiling monster
a heavy frog resting
water dripping down its mouth

is it trying to talk to you

or is it waiting for you
to sit and meditate on -

37.

Triggered by
great beauty
speechless gaps
short moments of
love, joy and peace
arising from
beyond the mind
beyond thinking

keep them going
realising there is
nothing else
no past and no future
only now -

38.

Surrounded by darkness
the light of a candle
the smell of ginger and tea
listening to the silence
right now
the presence
of now
knowing that this
is the only access to being
makes me smile

orchids in the window
fresh and green leaves
sucking up water through their cells
me, here, breathing in air
feeling aliveness of the body
vibrating pulsing warm
suddenly thankful -

39.

London plane seed ball
where does it come from
surrounded by beeches
looking around

suddenly the long trunk
in front of me
touching it
looking
energy flowing upward

up there
small yellow and green leaves
softly waving in the wind
shimmering autumn colours
vibrating energy
life -

40.

The big bang of the universe
splitting up in yin yang
the three forces
the five elements
down to the solar systems
the big dipper's bright light
down on the earth
heaven earth
and humans in between
small grains of sand
loved by the universe
listening
trying to get in touch
and climb the way
back up there -

41.

Heaven
the beauty of the dark lilac sky
lit up from beneath
from the city full of people
wonderful confused and wise people
a necklace of golden pearls
stretched out at the horizon
light that is mirrored
in the deep lilac sea

on the land the earth
down here a world
a microcosm of what is up there
our little wondrous world
walking on wet golden leaves
light reflected a thousand times
in the puddles

the words I love you
reduced to
but also upgraded to
I love
love -

42.

Winter approaching for real
afternoon light on autumn leaves
coldness in the air

church on a hilltop
bells blessing the country below
and all people

you are all blessed
you just may not know it
continuing busy lives
(traffic noise in the distance)
but look
the coldness clearness the beauty
all around you
is essence
is life -

43.

Driving by night
you can disappear into darkness
you can fall into a hole
a puddle bottomless
or - you can listen
to the rain
raindrops on their way
back under the skin
of the earth
dripping gurgling joining altogether
where they came from
and will rise from again
circulating
through darkness

you can be afraid
but you also can choose not to
you can trust the changing
of all things, move on and
be on the way to
become one -

44.

Behind the full moon
in the rustling of leaves
in the holes of a flute
in your eyes smile
behind an armchairs cushions
telling stories

there is
poetry

in a watering can forgotten on the terrace
in a garden chair worn by sun and rain
in the nice smell of blooming tea in my cup
in a falling leaf in front of the window

here it hides
poetry -

45.

Poetry
a secret thing

hiding the strangest places
where everything flows more slowly
on small footpaths
of rubble and sand
held together by leaves of grass
green oases
where oceans of time are
dropping leaves on the ground
talking to you
making patterns for you to read
the signs from
where there are small birds and animals
making you smile
by their presence

trust
that in being silent
you will gain -

46.

Bicycling
suddenly the picture of
my shadow moving along next to me
with every movement my body takes
bound together
it cannot stop
it cannot do anything else -

like this
the zen master says
the awareness
for everything
not seizing
not stopping
for a single moment
no gap!

47.

A smell of incense
a smell of innocence
and diving right into samadhi

turning inside
to a bursting empty body
vibrating at the edges
with atoms of light
this body breathes
every atom breathes -

sounds meeting no ear
colours meeting no eye
shining through without hindrance
being but not being

overflowing
just smiling
compassionate
for every single
living being -

48.

My friends
share with me this
in the spirit
in the mind

take from me as a sign
of gratitude and love
this sweet cake
and share with me
this bowl of matcha tea

let there be mutual understanding
and care for each other
all around the world -

49.

With new eyes
with pure eyes
a step outside
in a new world

cool wet air
a white wagtail dancing
after flies in the grass

just as it is
like that
nothing more
but how great -

V

Poems inspired by
Vladimir Megre's "Anastasia"
2010-2012

50.

Joy
the grass is growing
shining apple colour glowing
love
amidst every particle of air
vibrating
sent by the warming rays
of Anastasia -

51.

Anastasia

here are living farms and fences

cherry trees blooming as white clouds

and happy bright colours around

to greet us

to celebrate

the new coming spring

and life as a whole

white cows on green grass

celebrate by being

and all this joy is

what I see in all -

52.

Stream of light shining
stream of glistening consciousness

as glimpses of eyes meeting
hearts joyful joined
a long chain of human
bright experiences
smiling longing fulfilling
circling through the air

and then meeting again
in another beautiful world -

53.

A beautiful goddess
behind the counter
behind the desk of the airport
cleaning in the dull toilet rooms

thank you
for emitting the belief
that we all are capable of
fulfilling our dreams
and give the next generations
the tools to dream
their own dreams

we can do
so much -

54.

The sun goes down
and the day goes by
energies shifting to a more
subtle level
but do not worry
the sun also shines
on the other side of the world
even behind the clouds you might see
it shines
and is there for you
as soon as you need it

do you feel the mighty warmth
smiling in you?

you are the sun
and you can do it -

55.

That is how they felt
the old and wise
saying praise

out of total perception
having emptied themselves
and then seeing all with blank eyes
and a blank mind like a child
every leaf glistening fresh and green
every song of the birds
a big thank you, a big yes

out of this emptiness
comes praise
with your arms thrown into the air
to the sky, shouting out loud:
praise the whole world
this complete perfect creation
only once, only now it is
can you see it

then praise with me
nature, love and
co-creation!

56.

Regain your strength
refresh your mind
quench your spirit

lie down
and relax
close your eyes
remove yourself
into the silence inside you

listen
from this emptiness

create
by your own image
a space of love
a space of splendour
a place where you would go
to recover
and become whole

it may be a green glade
surrounded by trees
silent and full of scents
of flowers and bees

it may be at the sea
breathing in and out
with the waves

it may be something different
by your own choice

create
now
be in there
breath in and out
slowly and deep
and just be

When you´re ready
open your eyes
and come back -

57.

There is light
there is energy
there is beauty emerging
from the earth
unseen connections
of ideas, words and love
intelligence communicating
right here, in all of us
showing, reminding, warning us
saying:

live in balance with all around you
we are one
wake up to the subtle beauty
that is life
go back to nature

do it now
there is still time -

58.

A huge tree
communicates

all leaves communicate
the roots communicate with fungi
using earthly energies to live
giving birth to next generations
giving food and shelter
protecting from the rain
strength and greenness
this is coexistence
this is the right way to live
not to overuse, misuse
taking more than necessary

for that it communicates
this is the most important message
it says
the tree in me

take care -

59.

Riding high
on a wave of light
on this longest day
of summer
everything open and bright
everything most yang

like in a painting
surreal light
seen with a painters eyes
I thought they exaggerated
but they did not
like this is
the creation
seen with the heart
felt with the heart
and praised as holy
with hallelujah and a truthful
yes -

60.

Watching the clouds
suddenly feeling connection
with the earth and atmosphere
every water atom
part of the big picture
breathing in me, in here
and out there
nice and quiet
in and out

as a result
being thankful
to the clouds -

61.

Sometimes I don't recognise
the world around me
nothing touches me inside or rings a bell
people seem disconnected from the earth
and birds disappearing
there are no smells of nature, no sounds
integrity loosing its meaning -

but then I come to think
of the spiritual tribe in my life
for example
people from an eco-village I know
and send you a greeting
because where you live
there are sounds and smells
and light ideas of nature
caressing mother earth and healing
growing flowers and plants
building warm houses with love
real human beings, real life

and thank you
for that experience -

62.

When watching the clouds
moving by hastily
changing the scene
behind landscape and trees

when watching the leaves
glowing greenly
and you breath in

when you are the clouds
and trees and glowing light
life energy

then you are present
you are
you -

63.

I feel rich
when I see through the eyes
of the divine

just see through those eyes
just hear with those ears
then all you see is yours
yours is the beauty of the world
the light in the room
the bird flying by
the plants and trees
with all their details
yours is all the love
of the world

in each moment
fresh and new -

64.

Walk away from the main road
choose the smaller winding path
heading not away, but slower
to the same goal

on the slower road
there is more time
to observe
more time
for small miracles
to happen
and between miracles
small pockets of
eternity -

65.

Walking the path step by step
thinking of generations of knowledge
an image emerging of a circle of earth
a huge wheel turning
parting in four seasons, four directions
the hours of the day
lifted by a power unseen
but felt in every atom
of your body

from here comes inspiration
comes the urge to write, draw and sing
and even if thoughts, images and songs
have been thought and sung before
it has to happen again
in this generation
in every single being
in all of us -

66.

It is there
the secret
the sacred

it is there
in the grass-overgrown path
in every leaf of grass
in the horse on the field
and in the butterflies around

it is there
in the quietness lingering
between the leaves of the trees
the growing summer vegetation
soaked in it

it is there
to be breathed in
to be bathed in
to be with
to be in -

67.

A picture given generously
a hint a view
a memorable view

paradise is
and is shown green
as a valley light and warm
in the distance

the way to it however
is not walked to the end yet
but a promise it is

shown by an angel
transparent crystal-clear
through him the way is open
to the valley
to the divine -

68.

A mysterious jewel made of jade
called a merkaba
two green pyramids merged
are heaven and earth
one with the top up, one down
and where they meet in the middle
we are, humans are
perfection is

in a night dream they re-emerge
green becomes blue
in a dark transparent world
making these pyramids come alive
still apart but moving
floating and approaching each other

I recognise the forms
and help merging them
back into one to
become a merkaba
again -

69.

Another dream, or not a dream
an ancient jungle shaman
teaching music trance to his apprentices
one of them me

together we fly high
watching a buddha statue from above
his head in the treetops

and even higher suddenly
a bright atmosphere of rainbow colours
pulsating beams
emitted from a centre
contracting and expanding
breathing

lifting the eyes
I see that this centre
is but one of a billion
and I am told that this is
the secret structure
of the universe -

70.

Every moment has it
the secret
the sacred

take for example this indian summer sun
shining in low from the fields outside
its sunbeams bathing glasses with tea
on the table in the clear light of life

this moment
use it to look
from the outside to the inside
aware of both in the now
make space for the unknown

then it can illuminate everything
and atoms of ethereal pearls
will float on the surface of being
ready to take off
and thank you
for having taken
the time -

71.

Sunbeams falling on
green oolong tea leaves
piled up in a lidded bowl
the water extracting the essence
of high-mountain tea trees
the essence of the soil there
and the air and the spirit
of the people picking leaves
producing this elixir
of life
whose scent now
reaches my nose

but ends up lifting
my soul to heights
never known before -

72.

A pale golden liquor
a light roasted scent
a broad pattern of colours
in the leaves in the cup
a puzzle a patchwork of colours

which story would it tell
if we fully understood
that each drop is worth
its weight in gold
squeezing it out
this golden beverage

the excitement to drink
in a moment -

73.

Subtle changes in nature
the shifting of energy fields
throughout the whole year
perceived within
seen with a poetic mind
- wagashi*

prepare your mind to open
prepare your mind to see
really see eternity
in every moment's
small wonders
- wagashi

* confectionary used in the japanese tea-ceremony

74.

Is this being a poet

this silent morning full of fog
with siskins flying over
hawthorns spreading
over the meadows
and me breathless

garden people might appreciate it
bird people would
and plant lovers
they definitely would

but for me being here
so full of awe
by the nearly invisible
this yearning inside
this suffering
sweet and delicious
this longing

trying to put this into words
nearly tears me apart -

75.

There it is, the light
shining in through the windows
the backdoor is opened
then one step forward
and everything changes

green light lingers
on the grass between trees
a garden golden, Eden
the edges seamed with
cherries, apples and lilacs
dandelions and a tulip
yellow sprouts of enlightenment
in this state of consciousness

I need to breath this in
I own this garden for a moment
I am this garden for a moment
this garden does not exist
in time -

76.

Forest I ask you
may I enter your world
and take part in your charm
I won't hurt you
though my mere existence
as a human on this earth
already hurts you enough
firs are waving their arms
feeling the wind

but down here the quietness
of ferns and mossy wonders
let a world reside
where fairies dance at dawn
along this path
with green umbrellas
and leave an energy
so fragrant, thick and silent
that I can feel it
although I cannot see -

77.

I want to give you a gift

imagine looking up into the sky
blue and fresh
with fluffy white clouds drifting
silently and calm as if they knew
where they were going
- these clouds I give to you

imagine the lime trees underneath
with fresh buds soon ready for bees
full of sunlight, glowing green
- these trees I give to you

imagine finally the song of the blackbird
hidden somewhere in the midst of leaves
as the most beautiful of all
- this song I give to you

please enjoy -

78.

If you long for the ocean
underneath the small waves
then dive

if you want to find the rhythm
behind rhythms
the all-pervading pulse
then breathe

breathe as if your body was just a shell
full of air, extending and contracting

then listen to the heartbeat inside
and the beat of everything else
listen to the pauses in between
your breath extending to the stars

become the space in between stars
the space between atoms
the nothingness between things
and from there observe
and notice

a smile on your face -

79.

Reading Thomas Merton
and his insights

that everything is ours
but on one important condition
that it is all given
there is nothing that we can claim
and as soon as we try to take something
as it were our own
we lose your eden

and I look at the clouds
look at all the green around me
the house, the chair, the clothes
everything I surround myself with
including my body
and I die from all that
for a while -

80.

The other day
down in the woods
I talked to a snail
and watched her slowly
moving her house
across the sandy path

even when approaching
bigger stones
she proceeded
with unchanging speed
one millimetre after the other

and slowly but steadily
she reached the other side
she reached
her destination -

81.

Universe I ask
what are your visions, your dreams
for our future here on earth

show us a way
to express our love to you
and all elements, animals and plants

show us signs
of what you want us to do
to fulfil our being here, in detail

how to say thank you
to meadows, valleys and the rain
to rainbows, livegiving sunbeams

how to show our appreciation
for all these wonders
for all this poetry

of everyday life -

About

In 2003 the photographer Semko Balcerski held an
exhibition called "The Fragments of Life" at Øksne-
hallen, in Copenhagen, Denmark. It showed a
series of photographic "fragments", kaleidoscopes,
images printed on transparent film, mounted be-
tween 2 m high glass sheets of float glass.

Accompanying the photos, Danish writer and
graphic designer Ulla Conrad had created twelve
poems for the occasion. They were printed on
transparent film banners, hanging from the
ceiling, adding words to the images, and the ideas
behind the photo art. Themes were the beauty of
nature and the ungraspable human mind (part I).
The rest of the poems were created later, in 2003-
2012, and are a continuation of the same ideas,
inspired also by other poets and ideas (parts II-V).
The number of poems is 9x9, or 81, inspired by
the number of poems in the Chinese classic the
Tao Te Ching.

Photos by Semko Balcerski, www.semko.dk
Poems by Ulla Conrad, www.ullaconrad.com